Arabian Spirit

SPIRIT OF THE HORSE SERIES

Words By Betsy Sikora Siino

BOWTIE
PRESS

Images By Bob Langrish

For Michael and Christopher
—BSS

Ruth Berman, editor-in-chief
Nick Clemente, special consultant
Doug Kraus, designer

Library of Congress Cataloging-in-Publication Data

Siino, Betsy Sikora.
    Arabian spirit / words by Betsy Sikora Siino ; images by Bob
Langrish.
        p.   cm. -- (Spirit of the horse series)
    ISBN 1-889540-16-1
    1. Arabian horse.   I. Title.   II. Series.
SF293.A8S553   1998
636.1'12--dc21   97-32162
                                                                    CIP

The horses in this book are referred to as *he* or *she* in alternating chapters,
unless their gender is apparent from the activity discussed.

The photographs on pages 52 (© Jeff Janson) and 53 (© Rob Hess) are
courtesy of the International Arabian Horse Association.

BowTie™ Press
3 Burroughs
Irvine, California 92618

Manufactured in Singapore

First Printing May 1998
Second Printing September 2002
10 9 8 7 6 5 4 3 2

Table of Contents

C H A P T E R 1

Horses of the Ages..5

C H A P T E R 2

A Working Partnership...17

C H A P T E R 3

A Symphony of Freedom...29

C H A P T E R 4

The First Year..39

C H A P T E R 5

The Big Show...51

C H A P T E R 6

Epilogue: Kindred Spirit..59

Glossary...64

CHAPTER ONE

Horses of the Ages

Atlantis. The Valley of Kings. Pompeii. For centuries, humans have tracked the great mysteries of history. And for centuries, one of the great mysteries to elude such efforts is the origin of the Arabian horse.

Despite massive excavations beneath the desert sands of the region now known as Arabia, we have yet to discover the true story of this horse. Yet it was here that this child of the desert, her roots buried for all time beneath the forbidding desert sands, was first discovered by the humans also native to this land. And here her legend took hold.

This legend weaves the tale of the Arabian as not only the perfect horse, but the first horse, as well. Though this is not the only breed to claim that honor, there may be some truth to the rumor. Biblical folklore suggests that the Arabian may have been the horse chosen to represent *Equus* on Noah's Ark. (Several generations following the Flood, the Biblical mariner's great-great grandson Bax is credited with capturing the wild Arabian mare Baz, the alleged matriarch of the illustrious family of Arabian horses.) After forty days and forty nights of rain, the Arabian remained most comfortable within her arid native land. Fate dictated that the early Arabian belonged with the Bedouin nomads of that land, and there she stayed for thousands of years.

At the time of that relationship's conception, an estimated three thousand to four thousand years ago, the Arabian must have presented an earthshattering image to the parched and desperate eyes of the wandering nomads who first saw her standing as an oasis amid the sand, the sun, and the wind of this mystical corner of the world.

A deceptively small horse of surprisingly delicate build, what a treasure the Arabian was to become to those whose lives depended upon an ability to exist where the world was nothing but a wide expanse of sand baking beneath a searing sun. An Arabian who could travel great distances in intense heat on a minimum of fuel was more precious than gold to the nomadic peoples who first enlisted this animal as lifeline. Courageous and smart, ripe with heart and stamina, this horse provided the ultimate steed in both peacetime and at war; a dependable mode of transport for desert travel; and a delightful, not to mention

beautiful, companion in camp, where it was common for a cherished Arabian to pass the night sheltered safely within her family's desert tent.

Two thousand years ago, if one happened upon an encampment of such tents in a Middle Eastern desert, he or she might have witnessed a scene very much like one from the classic film epic, *Ben Hur*. En route to Jerusalem, Charlton Heston's Hur, a renowned charioteer, meets a Bedouin chieftain seeking a driver for his team of fine white Arabians. The horses are introduced to Hur as "my children," and are welcomed into the tent where the men are feasting. The proud host tells his visitor that the sheik would have brought the horses' mother, but his people simply would not tolerate her absence.

Another who could not bear the absence of the Arabian was seventh-century Islamic leader Mohammed, whose followers often spoke of "the five mares of the Prophet." According to legend, Mohammed once withheld food and water from his Arabian herd for three days. When at last he set them free to quench their thirst, he simultaneously sounded the call to battle. Five of the horses, five mares, stopped and answered the call, placing their loyalties to their master above their own needs. Mohammed in turn rewarded their obedience by deeming that these mares were the only mares who would be bred to carry on the line.

For centuries, this tale has inspired breeders of Arabian horses, evident in the great care nomadic Arabs took in the

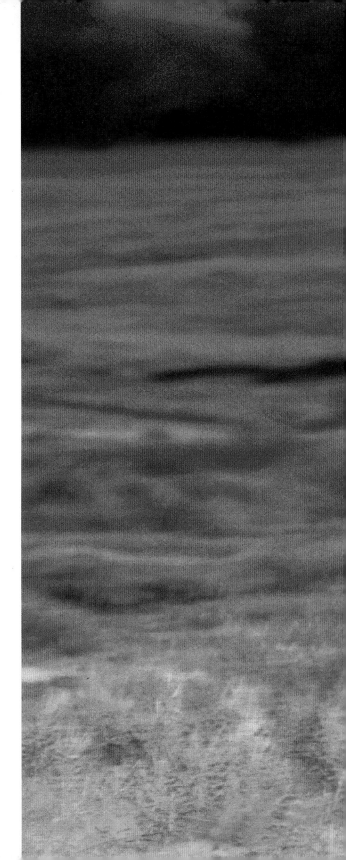

tracking and guarding of their horses' pedigrees. Self-taught experts in selective breeding practices, they insisted on breeding only those animals who exhibited the finest physical attributes and temperaments. One can only imagine the heated exchanges that occurred between these individuals as they met to arrange marriages, so to speak, that would influence the Arabian horse for hundreds, if not thousands, of years to come.

The divine offspring of such diligence were called by Mohammed to the seventh-century mission of spreading Islam throughout the then-known world. In promoting his lovely equine ambassador beyond the borders of Arabia, Mohammed convinced his followers that to care properly for one's horse was to earn a passport to

heaven. In the end, the results of the Islamic leader's efforts to gain converts to his faith paled against the mass conversions he inspired to the gifts of the Arabian horse.

In the wake of the Arabian's first forays beyond the realm of Aladdin, the call for Arabians resounded throughout the world. The call was answered, evident in the fact that today, from Great Britain to Spain, from Russia to eastern Europe to North America and beyond, all nations now proudly boast the presence of the legendary Arabian within their borders.

As her reputation swept into other nations, the Arabian's genetic makeup was viewed correctly as a precious commodity, not only for the continuation of her own kind, but for the refinement and enhancement of almost every other breed on the planet. The Thoroughbred, for one, owes his extraordinary physical gifts to Arabian influence, as do breeds as diverse as, among others, the Welsh pony, the Percheron, and the entire family of European warmbloods. Yet while her ancient blood has made profound contributions to virtually every other horse on earth, the Arabian has herself bred pure for three thousand, five thousand, perhaps even seven thousand years.

The Arabian never failed to stand out as premier warhorse on battlefields worldwide, adapting swiftly to new, undesertlike methods of warfare with skill and endurance. A beloved Egyptian-bred Arabian named Marengo fought with Napoleon and was captured at Waterloo. Another carried George Washington through the war that won America's independence. Ever nimble in their ability to evolve with the times, Arabians participated in both of the twentieth century's world wars, where they were prized both as cavalry mounts and as war spoils.

Indeed from the seventh century to the twentieth, warriors of all nations, all cultures, have never hesitated to praise their war mounts of either full or part Arabian breeding. In these horses they unabashedly invested more trust than they afforded their comrades in arms. At the same time, the horses, never shrinking from the call to battle, earned a reputation for bravery that made their great beauty seem all the more miraculous—and, in the heat of battle, downright insignificant.

CHAPTER TWO

A Working Partnership

When those in the horse world hear the term *working horse*, a specific image comes to mind: a large, heavy draft horse of cold-blood with a broad back, feathered feet, and a massive Roman head.

In the traditional sense, this indeed describes a working horse—a large cold-blood draft animal of quiet disposition, whose size is matched only by his strength. But this is by no means the only type of working horse. Just look at the Arabian. For thousands of years, this light-bodied, hotblooded animal has earned the right to claim the working title for himself, and he has succeeded quite handsomely in convincing our species just how valid that claim is.

Make the assumption that the Arabian is simply beauty without brains, intelligence, or

talent, and incite the wrath of this breed's passionate following throughout the world. From the very moment of his conception, from the appearance however long ago of this lovely creature on the earth, he has risen to the challenge of whatever calling was sent his way.

There is virtually no equine activity that we humans have conjured up that the Arabian will not at least attempt, and, in most cases, conquer. The breed's résumé would fill volumes, and in a sense it has. Documentation, if not of the Arabian's creation then certainly of his experiences since that time, abounds, and few would dare suggest that the great claims made about the Arabian are unwarranted.

And just why, we might ask, has the Arabian been so persistent in thrusting himself so willingly into any type of human and equine endeavor? Would it not have been simpler just to rest on the laurels of his breathtakingly good looks? To be adored and admired just because he came to earth as the quintessential prototype of equine beauty? Such a lifestyle, if afflicted upon this horse, is an insult to the animal's integrity, not to mention to the sharp intellect he has used for his benefit as well as our own for thousands of years. A life of pampered luxury? Not for the Arabian, thank you very much.

No, this horse is compelled to work, to spend his days in mutual effort with humans. This is no beast of burden, however. The Arabian demands a full and equal partnership with the people in his life. When granted this honor, the Arabian will work to earn the respect of all he encounters and will sacrifice heart and soul to achieve that.

Now that the grisly practice of man-to-man combat on horseback is an extinct phenomenon, contemporary times offer the Arabian decidedly more pleasant pursuits in which he may exhibit his skills. On any given weekend anywhere in the world, spectators may be treated to exhibitions of the Arab's ancient work ethic in competition venues, the horses exhibiting the fruits of a foundation built on centuries of hard work and camaraderie with humans.

Thanks to that foundation, today with ease Arabians are springing up and over oxers in jumping competitions; they are

chasing tiny balls tirelessly around polo courses in a game resembling soccer on horseback; and with elegance and grace, they are performing the moves of classical horsemanship in the intricate ballet that is dressage. Arabians are transporting their riders safely over fallen trees on forested cross-country courses. They are crossing the finish line of Arabian races, convincing their ardent fans that if pitted against Thoroughbreds on a track longer than that to which the blood horse is accustomed, the Arabian would surely emerge victorious. They are strutting their lovely stuff pulling carts in flashy driving competitions, and they are spinning pirouettes in the western reining arena, stopping on a dime in response to their riders' unseen signals to change directions.

Yet to witness the twentieth-century calling for which the Arabian's desert heritage has most eloquently prepared him, one must look to the wilderness. The treacherous, seemingly endless, mountain trails would make many, if not most, horses stop in their tracks, turn around, and head back to the barn. But to the healthy, well-conditioned Arabian, home is where the endurance course is. Few equine vocations are as demanding as the sport of endurance, and few horses are as perfectly equipped for the job as is the Arabian.

Forty miles. Fifty miles. One hundred miles. Endurance competitions require a horse to take such treks in a single day. Only the cream of the crop need apply, and only the cream is chosen, as only those horses with the proper conditioning are given the green light to compete in endurance. The dominance of the Arabian in this field is testament to the breed's natural ability in this area, and to the historical vocations that led to his contemporary success.

Rare is the rider who has experienced the rigors of endurance riding, a school rooted in a military tradition designed to test the mettle of military horses. Though now launched as a more pleasurable endeavor, the test remains tough. The steep grades. The obstacle-laden trails. The porcelain

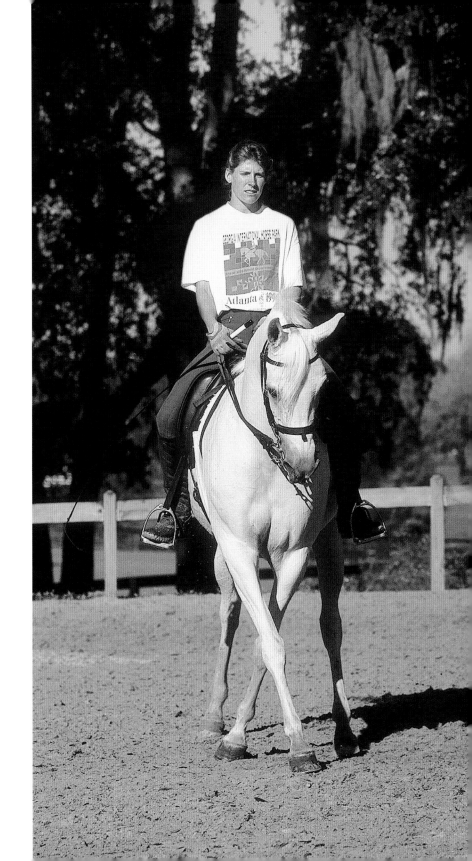

sound of hoof slipping on rock beneath water. The jolt of a sudden stumble that brings a hot flush to the rider's cheeks. The recurring thought that just around that turn—that's got to be the end.

How does one quite describe the immense rewards of tackling that challenge together with a horse who has made it his mission to take care of the rider on his back? The Bedouins understood the fullness of the heart, the blinked-back tear in the eye, the swelling in the throat that could only be inspired by such an accomplishment—and by such a horse.

The obvious bond between the endurance horse and his rider is often more riveting than the actual athletic feat itself. All one must do is imagine being stationed at one of the designated rest stops set up to monitor the horses in an endurance competition. Enter into the clearing a slender, well-muscled Arabian gelding with fire in his eyes and large nostrils flared, the spring in his gait evidence that he can easily handle the many miles yet to come. His rider, her face aglow with sweat and exhilaration, dismounts, pulls a stethoscope from a saddle bag, and gauges the horse's pulse and respiration. Of course the event veterinarian, whose job is to determine which horses will continue and which must stop, will do the same, but this rider trusts only her own evaluations of her trusted mount's welfare.

Quietly the rider waters the horse. Gently stroking his forelock as he drinks, she whispers soft words meant only for his ears.

Finally she places her helmet back on her head, checks the girth of the saddle and remounts. The two vanish into the trees to face an unknown set of obstacles and an acknowledged treacherous terrain. In the end, it matters not if they "win." The winning is in their pursuing this grand challenge as a team, guided by a mutual, and very ancient, respect between horse and human.

But an Arabian need not be a topflight endurance champion to pay homage to the working legacy left by his ancestors. This he does in every activity he undertakes, including the activity of companion. Outside of the realm of competition, in a job just as important as that of the full-time athlete, Arabians are simply enjoying human company every day, carrying trusted riders on local trails, reveling in the ministrations of the daily grooming routine, and participating in training sessions that help to hone their ancient energies. Whether in formal showing or pleasure activities, the natural affection the Arabian has for human beings is evident in his every response to the familiar human voice and every spark of interest incited by the introduction of some new and exciting adventure.

So that is why the Arabian works so hard. That is why he spends his life striving to please his human partners. This horse likes us, that's all. Why he likes us so is just another of this mysterious animal's secrets, the answer to which he will never divulge.

CHAPTER THREE

A Symphony of Freedom

I magine an Arabian mare running at
pasture on a warm spring day. Ecstasy
spurring the horse on, the spectator can't
help but imagine this animal back in her
ancestral homeland, floating across the white
sands of her desert domain, nostrils flared,
muscles rippling, lush mane and tail flying
like a delicate veil in the wind.

It is precisely this vision that artists have
for centuries attempted to capture in their
works. From ancient and rather primitive
sculptures depicting dish-faced horses in
various states of movement, to more
contemporary renditions of prized Arabian
stallions at war and sport, artists of every age
have striven to capture that magic in stone,
clay, tapestry, oils—anything that can be
manipulated into an imitation of reality.

What this grand artistic tradition has left us is an impressive visual chronicle that immortalizes for all time the arched neck; the lustrous mane and tail; the wide forehead offset by dark, luminous eyes and small curved ears; the large nostrils that so efficiently enhance the horse's respiration and stamina; and the distinguishing concave profile of the Arabian horse. At the same time, the antiquity of these pieces, and the uniformity of the images they present, provide the world with a unique historical record composed of works from regions as diverse as Russia, China, England, Poland, and ancient Greece and Rome, proving that the Arabian has changed very little through the centuries.

The horse who has remained so steadfast in type and demeanor for millennia, is a beautiful, though relatively small animal who rarely exceeds 15.2 hands in height, but who harbors immense power and muscle within her small frame. A most prominent component in the Arabian's signature appearance is the dished profile, the *afras*, the trademark broad forehead and delicate muzzle made all the more lovely by the horse's large, wide-set eyes and pert, petite ears.

Found in virtually every color of the equine rainbow, the Arabian is known for a soundness of structure borne of centuries of selective breeding to ensure only the finest horses carried on the line. That structure itself sets the Arabian apart from other

breeds, this horse having one less rib, two fewer tail bones, and, in many cases, one less lumbar vertebra than other horses have. The breed's short, slightly concave back, coupled with hard feet, overall balance, and strong, well-proportioned legs, propel the horse forward with speed, stamina, elegance, and an action that is most accurately described as floating.

As beautiful and sensitive as she is athletic, the Arabian pioneered the concept

of horses as companions and family members. In keeping with this at-one-time-revolutionary notion, our words as well as our artistically drawn images reflect without fail the universal attributes of the breed that translate to all cultures, all levels of society. A poll of people who knew the horse one thousand years ago would no doubt evoke a chorus of responses echoing those heard today in every language, from every nation, in praise of this magnificent beast.

Within this century, we find that chorus reflected in literature celebrating the Arabian, from Marguerite Henry's *King of the Wind* to Walter Farley's *The Black Stallion.* We find

kings, queens, heiresses, aristocrats, captains of industry, and showbiz types all enamored of the Arabian horse. But so do we find so-called regular folks, who are just as devoted and just as privileged to be living with Arabians each and every day of their lives.

Bold. Intelligent. Sensitive. Clairvoyant. Athletic. That is the Arabian. We thus cannot help but look to that lovely animal running at pasture, imagining the joy of running with her, racing with abandon, together paying homage to the sun. Whether immortalized in stone, on canvas, in the spoken or written word, or simply in the mind's eye, the Arabian touches the artist within us all.

The First Year

With the exception perhaps of the rather mysterious origins of that first Arabian, every Arab begins his adventure on earth in the very traditional role as foal.

When one chooses to breed an Arabian, he or she accepts the torch from all the devoted breeders who have come before, and must therefore agree to proceed with only the purest of hearts. This dedicated breeder allows the inspiration of the first masters to guide his or her more contemporary efforts, evaluating with great care the prospective sire and dam to ensure that only the finest are allowed to contribute to the living history of the Arabian horse.

Imagine the thrill when the dream is finally realized. After all the uncertainty,

effort, and worry, the tiny foal arrives, pulls himself up on spindly legs, and looks around with a dazed expression of wonderment in his large, doelike eyes. This wobbly animal represents the best and brightest of the newest generation of Arabians.

All foals come into the world in much the same way, but Arabian foals arrive with an inner magic that even veteran breeders have difficulty defining. They just know it when they first spot the newborn's large eyes and the *jibbah*, the wide signature forehead bulge that marks almost every Arabian foal and was once thought to indicate a brain capacity superior to that of all other horses. While the Arabian's brain is in fact no larger, the challenge of caring constructively for this

newborn of such ancient breeding can be daunting to those unaccustomed to working with horses of extreme intelligence and hot-blooded energy.

Of course the foal's dam is perfectly up to this task. The unique maternal traditions of the Arabian world are grounded in the mare's natural callings to motherhood. But given the affection most of her kind harbor for the human species, the new mother should welcome the intervention of her most trusted human family members in this grand mission. Mom will be convinced of good intentions by the individual who behaves respectfully, handles both her and her foal gently, and speaks in hushed tones.

Such decorum is critical to the foal, who has been thrust after eleven months of

warmth and security within Mama's womb into a strange and noisy world where he is expected to stand up and in many ways fend for himself. Sure Mom is nearby, but also present in the stall are these two-legged creatures who in no way resemble anything equine, and whose scents seem so foreign from Mom's. The foal has no way of understanding that those two-legged creatures have an important mission at hand. It is their job to make the foal's initial experiences with the world positive, charging the youngster with the confidence and security required to face new experiences, not with fear, but with the courage and aplomb for which his breed is known.

If this foal is fortunate, his human handlers will be practitioners of imprinting, an avenue by which the newborn animal bonds to the first, shall we say, authority figures he encounters. Quietly they will approach the youngster and gently stroke his ears, his neck, his back, his feet, all the while allowing the foal to grow accustomed to their scents. They may even place a tiny halter on the foal's head for a few moments to convince the newborn in a positive manner that like these people, the halter is to become a part of his daily existence.

While there is great satisfaction to be had from nurturing an Arabian from foal to talented, well-trained adult, the Arabian is a breed slow to mature. The first ride and the under saddle training that follows should not begin until on or around the youngster's third birthday to ensure the bones of his legs have

fully developed. Nevertheless, there is much to be done during the early months.

The first year is a time to introduce and acclimate the foal to this wild and wonderful place that is now his home. In the process, the Arabian's hot blood, evident even during the youngster's first months, must be tamed and channeled with gentle consistency to set the stage for his future training and career.

All training, whether easing a foal's fear of the flapping edges of a desert tent or convincing the youngster, usually when he reaches about four or five months of age, that he no longer requires his mother's milk to thrive, must be done in the most positive fashion. This ancient, trusting soul, even at a tender, impressionable age, will not live up to his fullest potential if handled roughly or according to tenets of punishment rather than reward.

Introduce the young animal to the buzz of the clippers, the pressure of the hoof pick, the tug of the lead rope on the halter, and the tickle of fingers on the ears. Expose the animal to trees, dogs, children, cars, other horses, sirens—all the sights and sounds he is likely to encounter in the years to come both as pet and as athlete. Proceed with patience and a positive demeanor, and such enthusiasm will surely prove contagious to the foal.

Honor the youngest Arabian's profound sensitivity to the human voice, the human touch and the possibilities they represent, and touch the ancient affection for humans that waits there. This is the common thread that unites all Arabians in their collective consciousness, sprung from a dramatic, often bloody, always passionate heritage. Those who succeed in this grand mission gain admittance to an ancient club open only to those of the purest intentions.

The Big Show

Every year come October, a celebration occurs. Alternating each year between Albuquerque, New Mexico, and Louisville, Kentucky, it is the U.S. National Arabian and Half-Arabian Championship Horse Show. From all fifty states, more than two thousand horses congregate for this nine-day extravaganza, which, like so many other similar events held annually worldwide, showcases in concentrated fashion just what this consummate athlete, the Arabian, is all about.

The Arabian's show tradition is a long and respected one, its function grounded in the various and sundry historical callings of this horse. Theoretically, the horse who exhibits extraordinary skills in the show ring is the horse best equipped to live up to genuine responsibilities in the so-called real world. Even a touch of potent Arab blood packs a powerful wallop that is often all a horse needs to claim the blue ribbon. What ignites that blood is the legendary mutual partnership between Arab and owner, the latter of whom is ever compelled to show off just what his or her horse can do.

Sponsored by the International Arabian Horse Association, the Arabian Nationals provide an opportunity for owners, breeders, trainers, competitors, and just plain Arabian lovers to celebrate the breed's beauty and profound work ethic within a venue saturated in Arabians and Arabian lore. Here, those passionate about the breed can gather and both participate in and witness almost one hundred English, western, and every other

kind of class that showcases this breed's unmatched versatility.

The event has come a long way from the first national show in 1933 that hosted only forty-five horses vying for $150 in prize money. With entries now numbering in the thousands, and prize money totaling more than $1 million, there remains no doubt that the Arabian is one of the most powerful equine forces in the United States and in the world at large.

What has not changed is the excitement in the air at the Nationals, and the gusto with which participants, spectators, and horses all greet the challenge of celebrating the breed in an all-Arabian show setting. In this the Super Bowl of the Arabian world, the competition could not be more fierce—and everyone knows it.

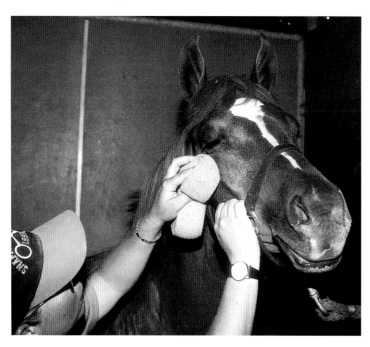

All one needs to do is stroll through the grounds and feel the electricity in the air. Backstage, the almost quarter of a million spectators who attend the event will see Arabians of every color; revel in the warm, comforting scent of horse; and listen to the symphony of whinnies that carry as an a cappella chorus through the crisp fall air.

The stakes are high, and the anxiety is evident. Each rider, each driver, each handler, like the Bedouin chieftain readying for battle, summons his or her own personal methods to prepare psychologically for that crucial moment before the judge, knowing that the first impression is the impression that counts. No weakness. No fear. To let the anxiety show could undermine contagiously the confidence of a horse as sensitive to human emotion as the Arabian.

But the anxiety reigns nonetheless. The incessant brushing of the tail, the braiding of the mane, the spontaneous embrace of a horse's neck, each act is a ritual designed to cement the bond that will soon be tested under the glaring lights of the arena and expectant eyes of those hungry to witness the Arabian in all its glory.

There is great beauty and great tradition in those rituals. Soon to be called into the ring, an elegantly turned out English pleasure competitor pats the thick French knot of hair at the back of her head and flicks an imaginary speck of dust from the shoulder of her tailored coat. A hunt seat rider on a gleaming chestnut holds the reins in trembling hands and prays that just this once

the horse will sprout wings and carry them both high above every jump in their path. A dressage competitor taps the toe of her boot repeatedly on the ground as an unconscious reflex, once again rehearsing today's pattern in her head. Meanwhile, a young woman, dwarfed by the intricately tooled saddle in her lap, polishes the silver ornamentation in preparation for the western pleasure class.

Spot a particularly large crowd and that will no doubt be the minions gathered to watch the ever-popular halter horses being prepared for their moment in the spotlight. Here the grooming reaches a fever pitch for this, the beauty pageant of breed competition. Naked for all the world to see, the horses will soon be paraded in front of the judges, who will evaluate how well they meet the Arabian ideal in structure, temperament, and conformation. According to the theory that function follows form, those horses who most closely meet the ideal should be the horses most ideally suited for work and breeding.

In the midst of all these oh-so-very-contemporary activities, yet another source of fascination unfolds. Preparing to enter the ring waits a contingent of Arabic warriors, dressed in flowing robes, their horses decked in tasseled bridles and ornate Arabic saddles. The native costume class is at hand, transporting everyone—horses, riders, and spectators alike—back in time to an era when the Arabian shared the tent of the Bedouin chieftain, and was still the desert's best-kept secret.

With more than twelve thousand Arabian foals being registered by the Arabian Horse Registry of America each year in the United States—and thousands more worldwide—we are not likely to return to that time of the Bedouin chieftain within our own age. But that does not mean we need ignore the Arab's influence on our imaginations, yet another skill at which the Arabian horse has always excelled.

Epilogue: Kindred Spirit

Just why the Arabian horse is as deeply bonded as he is to the human species is a mystery, pure and simple. That we in turn feel a kindred bond to this horse is no mystery at all.

How can we help but cherish this animal who has for centuries shared with us a symbiotic relationship that we might otherwise never believe could exist between horse and human? With the Arab, anything is possible—and always has been.

From the moment that first Arabian appeared on this planet, the horse world was forever changed. It is safe to say that without the Arabian, the horse simply would not be the animal it is today. The appearance, the intellect, the action, even the bone and muscle of almost every breed on earth would

not have evolved precisely as they have. That is quite a testament to the Arabian's influence, and to the power of his potent genes. But the Arabian has influenced us humans as well, not with an infusion of genetic material, but with his presence in our lives.

A most democratic animal in both his appeal and his affections, the Arabian has succeeded in crossing all cultural, religious, and economic boundaries simply by remaining true to who he is and who he was

Chapter Six

meant to be. This horse enchanted us thousands of years ago and he enchants us still, perhaps because we know that with an Arabian by our side, we are somehow made complete, somehow enhanced by this magnificent animal's presence. This wise old soul's affection for us, his loyalty to our kind, somehow convinces us of our own value. What fortunate souls we are to share our planet with such an animal.

Glossary

blood horse: a horse who is descended from purebred stock

cold-blood: a type of horse who is a heavy draft breed with a calm and passive temperament descended from the large forest horses of northern Europe

draft horse: a strong horse, powerfully built, who is bred and used for pulling heavy loads or for farm work

dressage: a form of exhibition riding in which the horse receives nearly invisible cues from the rider and performs a series of difficult steps and gaits with lightness of step and perfect balance. Dressage also is a classical training method that teaches the horse to be responsive, attentive, willing, and relaxed for the purpose of becoming a better equine athlete.

halter horse: an unsaddled horse led into a show ring in a halter to be judged for conformation and condition

hand: a standard of equine height measurement derived from the width of a human hand. Each hand equals 4 inches, with fractions expressed in inches. A horse who is 16.2 hands is 16 hands, 2 inches, or 66 inches tall at the withers.

hotblood: a high-spirited and active horse descended from Middle Eastern or North African ancestors

hunt seat: A style of English riding, suited for horses who are hunters and jumpers, based on traditions in the hunt field. In a variety of show classes, hunters are judged on style and manners as they go over jumps, while jumpers are judged on their ability to get over tough obstacles without knocking them down.

oxer: a jump made of two separate elements of a fence that are jumped as one

pedigree: the recorded list of a horse's ancestors

selective breeding: breeding intended to encourage specific traits such as coat color, temperament, or size

under saddle: A class in hunt seat that judges the horse on good manners and form as he walks, trots, and canters. There is no jumping involved.

warmblood: a term used to describe distinct breeds usually named according to the region in which the breed was developed. These large, well-muscled horses possess the calm temperament of their cold-blood draft ancestors and the athleticism of their hotblood forebears, making them suitable for dressage and show jumping.